MOJADA

BY LUIS ALFARO

DRAMATISTS PLAY SERVICE

MUSIC AND THIRD-PARTY MATERIALS USE NOTE

IMPORTANT BILLING AND CREDIT REQUIREMENTS

The New York premiere of MOJADA was produced by the Public Theater (Oskar Eustis, Artistic Director; Patrick Willingham, Executive Director) in July 2019. It was directed by Chay Yew, the set design was by Arnulfo Maldonado, the costume design was by Haydee Zelideth, the lighting design was by David Weiner, the sound design was by Mikhail Fiksel, and the production stage manager was Buzz Cohen. The cast was as follows:

MEDEA .... Sabina Zúñiga Varela
JASON .... Alex Hernandez
ACAN .... Benjamin Luis McCracken
TITA .... Socorro Santiago
PILAR .... Ada Maris
LUISA .... Vanessa Aspillaga

The West Coast premiere of MOJADA was first performed at the Getty Villa, Los Angeles, California, on September 10, 2015. It was directed by Jessica Kubzansky, the set design was by Efren Delgadillo Jr., the costume design was by Raquel Barreto, the lighting design was by Ben Zamora, the original music and sound design were by Bruno Louchouarn, and the production stage manager was Jaclyn Kalkhurst. The cast was as follows:

MEDEA .... Sabina Zúñiga Varela
HASON .... Justin Huen
ACAN .... Anthony Gonzalez and Quinn Marquez
TITA .... Vivis
JOSEFINA .... Zilah Mendoza
ARMIDA .... Marlene Forte

The world premiere of MOJADA was produced by Victory Gardens Theater (Chay Yew, Artistic Director; Christopher Mannelli, Managing Director), Chicago, Illinois, in July 2013. It was directed by Chay Yew, the set design was by Yu Shibagaki, the costume design was by David Hyman, the lighting design was by Heather Gilbert, the sound design was by Mikhail Fiksel, and the production stage manager was Tina M. Jach. The cast was as follows:

MEDEA .... Sandra Delgado
JASON .... Juan Francisco Villa
ACAN .... Ricky Reyes and Dylan Lainez
TITA .... Socorro Santiago
JOSEFINA .... Charin Alvarez
ARMIDA .... Sandra Marquez

BRUJA, a first adaptation of *Medea*, was commissioned, developed, and received its world premiere in 2012 by Magic Theatre (Loretta Greco, Producing Artistic Director), San Francisco, California. It was directed by Loretta Greco, the set design was by Andrew Boyce, the costume design was by Alex Jaeger, the lighting design was by Eric Southern, the sound design was by Jake Rodriguez, and the production stage manager was Julie Haber. The cast was as follows:

MEDEA .... Sabina Zúñiga Varela
JASON .... Sean San José
ACAN .... Daniel Castaneda/Daniel Vigil
ACAT .... Gavilan Gordon-Chavez/Mason Kreis
VIEJA .... Wilma Bonet
CREON .... Carlos Aguirre
AEGEUS .... Armando Rodriguez

CHARACTERS

MEDEA, 20s

JASON, 30s

ACAN, 10

TITA, 60s

JOSEFINA, 30s

ARMIDA, 50s

All of the characters are Mexican.

MOJADA

Prologue

Summer in the yard of a house in Boyle Heights, old-world, maybe ancient. The backdrop is a typical two-story old Victorian, way past her prime, but unique in her blend of wood and brick.

The furniture, a rustic wooden table, potted plants of herbs and vegetables are unmistakably Mexican. A little table houses a portable sewing machine connected to extension cords that snake through the yard and into the house, a milk crate in the corner.

We hear an ancient sound, something sustained.

A mother and son, Medea and Acan, can be seen up on a landing. She holds him in her arms. They begin a dance, something ancient; it is clear she is teaching him a ritual. It is joyful, playful, and full of love. Maybe funny even.

Tita, a viejita, worn but enduring, enters the yard and goes to the garden, pulling a pair of very large discarded banana palms. Medea and Acan reach for banana palms as well. She stands in the center of the yard and conjures as she holds the banana leaves in each hand, gripping them as if they were talons or wings. She holds them up to the sky as all three sing a prayer in Nahuatl.

As they slap the palms together, they produce the sound of "back there," and there goes Tita in her memories; Slap—the sound of the old country. Slap—a party with music. Slap— rain. Slap—lovers making love. Slap—a baby crying. Slap— a woman laughing. Slap—the sound of a bird, in flight, wings flapping. Medea and Acan listen for the sound as well.

TITA. *Buenas tardes! I SAID, BUENAS TARDES! That's better.* So, who has the gossip?

Back home, I see a *vecina* on the street and I say, "*Oye, mujer,* your husband, he looks like a bull, does he make love like one too?" And she says, "Yes he does!" But here, if I ask about the bull, they say, "*Ai,* how can you ask that, and on the street too, *vieja sin vergüenza!*" As if I ask to see the bull in action!

They hide their *chisme* here because someone always wants to steal your secrets, your smile, your bull. That is why it is better to have nothing in this country, which is exactly what I have.

The sewing machine begins. We hear Medea humming to herself.

Yo soy Tita. Here, they tell me, "Oh—housekeeper," but back home, I am family. I cook, I clean, I shop, I take the boy to school and pick him up, right?

Acan nods his head.

And sometimes, I buy him some American candy when he is good, but today, no candy, right?

Acan nods his head again.

This is a lot of work for a woman of my age, but, you know, family… I have been with her since she was born. I came to her *familia* as a *niña* myself. Her mother dies in childbirth, the men need their meals, and she needs someone to raise her, to teach her the old ways. I was sold to her family with a herd of cattle and a little goat. That was the first thing they ate. I had no idea he was food, I thought he was my friend, *pero* he was delicious…

I am a *curandera,* a healer. We rub, we touch, we look inside you. Everything I know I have taught *mi* Medea, but her gift is *en las manos*… Here they think she is just a seamstress, but what she does with the cloth and the pattern and the sewing is *puro pinche* da Vinci.

Late at night they deliver stacks of fabrics. They say, "No name, no social, we pay you cash. You complain, we go to someone else." They check her seams, her hems, and they are always *muy* impressed, but they can't show it, because then…

> *She does a gesture for money.*

Welcome to the factory inside your house.

Back home she is an artist, *la reina del vestido*, here she is a sewing machine. In this country, you can only be one thing; here or there, lost or found, man or woman, but back there we have—*en medio*. Like me, I smile, but I hate you…

> *She looks at the audience with the most hateful smile.*

I know, I know, you thinking, "Why is she so unhappy?" I am not unhappy, I am a senior citizen! And I have so much to do. And my time is not long. She is not well. I need to get her out of the house. This is Jason, her husband's dream, not ours. She will do anything for him. He is her first and her last, she says. *Ai que mensa!*

What is going to become of us? I hardly cook anymore. It's all McDonald's *por aqui*. *Pero*, I will stay with her until I die. If she dies before me, I will jump into her grave, and they can bury us both. These things do not matter to me. I say, better to die with *mi niña* than to live with nothing to do.

> *We hear a call in the distance, the sound of a bird…*

JASON. *(Offstage.) Gwa, Gwa, Gwa…*

> *Medea looks up, hearing it. Acan runs toward the sound. Tita hears it too and moves toward her milk crate.*

TITA. *Pinche* bird…

ACAN. *Papi!*

> *Acan appears at the top of the stairs.*

Papi!

> *Jason enters. A cell phone to his ear, he motions for Acan to come down the stairs, where he hugs him. He kicks the ball and the boy runs off after it.*

One

JASON. *(Speaking on his cell.)* No, no, no, don't you worry. Figueroa will go off without a hitch, missus. We have it all under control, the Orsinis are the same apartment, we just copy the last one.

> *Jason laughs and Tita copies his laugh as she rolls her eyes, under her breath…*

TITA. *Idiota…*

> *Jason glares at her.*

JASON. I will. And once again, thank you for everything, missus.

> *He smiles.*

Oh! Well thank you… *(Suddenly shy.)* I would love to…

> *Jason hangs up, turns to look at Medea sewing and goes to her.*

TITA. "You would love to" what?

JASON. Mind your own business, *chismosa!* *(To Medea.)* How is my *guaco?*

MEDEA. I feel like a bird who has lost her feathers.

JASON. I thought I was the only one.

MEDEA. *Gwa!* *(Noticing his shoes.)* Where did you get those shoes?

JASON. You notice everything, the old lady taught you well.

TITA. *Callate pendejo.*

JASON. That *vieja's* tongue, I swear to God!

MEDEA. *Dejalo Tita!*

TITA. *Baboso!*

MEDEA. *Tita!* *(Back to the issue at hand.)* Entonces?

JASON. They bought them for me.

MEDEA. Who did?

JASON. My job.

MEDEA. A job buys you shoes? We haven't even been here a year.

JASON. My boss.

> *He spits out a loogie.*

MEDEA. *Ai, Jason!*

TITA. *Que romantico!*

JASON. *Callate, viejita* nosy.

MEDEA. It's disgusting.

JASON. Then you must love a disgusting man, because this is what men do, I am only following the rules.

MEDEA. Is that what you are going to do when you get promoted?

JASON. When I get promoted I will go to CVS and buy a handkerchief like Villaraigosa, but I promise you that when no one is looking, Villaraigosa is spitting too. Are you almost done?

MEDEA. I will never be done, it's all collars and cuffs, twice the work. You know how much they sell this for over at the, what did you say it was…

TITA. …Bloomingdale's…

MEDEA. Tell him what they told you.

TITA. One hundred and twenty dollars…

MEDEA. I get eight dollars for making it. And look, I got myself good today.

> *She unpeels a bandage and shows him her finger. He kisses it.*

I had to do three hundred pieces twice over because they changed their mind on the stitch. When we complained, he told Tita he could take the work somewhere else.

JASON. What did you say?

TITA. We will do them again.

MEDEA. And I smiled. How did I smile Tita?

> *Tita smiles her "I hate you" smile.*

JASON. Don't smile at them.

MEDEA. They don't come back otherwise.

JASON. What you do is special, Medea, no matter how they treat us here.

MEDEA. In this country, special pays the same.

JASON. I promise that when I am in charge, my wife is going to stay home and get fat and make me *tamales* all day, real ones made with lard.

MEDEA. I thought you wanted us to look more American?

JASON. And you, old lady, will mix *la masa* just so you can know what it feels like to do labor.

TITA. I work!

JASON. Is that what they call gossiping these days?

TITA. When we go back to Michoacán I am going to get a job better than this one, as a *puta*!

MEDEA. Tita!

> *They can't help but laugh.*

JASON. I am going to take the boy to the pier.

MEDEA. There's a pier?

JASON. At the ocean, Medea! In Santa Monica, it has a big Ferris wheel. Two metros to get there.

MEDEA. Really?

JASON. We are all going to go, this weekend.

TITA. *Yo tambien?*

JASON. Yes, you too, old lady.

> *Jason turns to look at Medea.*

MEDEA. You know I can't go.

JASON. I don't know that.

MEDEA. We'll see…

JASON. Medea, *por favor*. We've been here almost a year, and we haven't gone anywhere. For the boy.

MEDEA. *(Feeling trapped.)* I don't know… It seems far.

JASON. *Mi reina*, how do you know how far it is?

MEDEA. It's on the other side of the buildings, right?

JASON. *(Looking at Tita.)* Tell her it's not that far.

TITA. Only two metros, Medea. And they're clean!

JASON. At least leave the house, Medea! We can't keep depending on the old lady for everything.

TITA. See, I work!

JASON. *Callate!* Seriously Medea…

MEDEA. I don't know…

She goes back to sewing, but he puts his arms around her.

JASON. I am putting my foot down. We are going to go to the beach as a family!

MEDEA. *(An outburst.)* NO! I CAN'T!

Whoa, where did that come from? Tita stands.

JASON. Okay, okay… I am sorry. It was too much to ask. I'll take the boy myself. I was hoping… I just… I'll make it better, Medea. I will.

They are interrupted by the chifle *of Acan whistling down the street. Medea goes inside the house. Tita stands to go with her, but Medea nods for her to stay. Tita and Jason look at each other as Tita sits at her milk crate.*

Two

A soccer ball rolls into the yard as Jason goes for it, followed by Acan dressed in a fútbol *soccer outfit with a homemade jersey emblazoned with the name Chicharito on the back.*

ACAN. *Papi!*

Jason does tricks with the ball and kicks it to Acan.

JASON. Call me DAD.

ACAN. What's the difference?

JASON. That's the way they say it here.

ACAN. But you're *Papi.*

JASON. It's the same thing, but here in this country it sounds like this… *(In a tough-guy voice.)* DAD! See? It's strong. *(Mimics Acan's voice.)* Papi! See? That sounds like a duck that's lost in a pond. *(Doing the tough-guy again.)* DAD! It makes you sound like a man.

ACAN. DAAAD!

JASON. Yeah, like that.

> *Jason picks up Acan and spins him around. They laugh as he puts him down and points to his jersey.*

Where is your Donovan?

ACAN. *Mami* said I could only wear Mexico.

> *Jason's cell gets a text.*

JASON. We'll see about that.

ACAN. Can I have one?

JASON. What?

ACAN. A cell.

JASON. What do you need a cell for?

ACAN. So I can call you.

JASON. We're never apart.

ACAN. We could be if you bought me a cell.

JASON. Acan, you are my future, we will never be apart. Now let's get you into something a little more American. But don't tell your *mami*…

> *They kick the soccer ball to each other. Finally, Jason kicks the soccer ball off towards the front of the house and Acan runs after it while Jason leaves, checking his cell.*

Three

> *Tita picks up a large, rusted machete as she stares at the banana tree. Medea enters, surprised by her.*

MEDEA. *Ai, Tita!*

TITA. Ooh sorry sorry, it's just that this *pinche* banana tree, I keep pruning and feeding *y nada.*

MEDEA. It's too dry here. It's not going to give off any fruit, let it remind us of Zamora.

> *Medea goes to the sewing machine and begins to work.*

TITA. It refuses to settle here as much as you and I…

The sound of a helicopter, Tita looks up at it as it passes.
Jason didn't come home…

MEDEA. He has to work all night. There are a lot of Orsinis.

TITA. What do you know about Orsinis?

MEDEA. Lots of apartments, they will take advantage of him before they reward him, that's the way it works.

TITA. And you believe him?

MEDEA. Why wouldn't I?

TITA. Everyone else goes home to sleep.

MEDEA. He is not everyone else, he is going to be the boss. He is showing them what he is willing to do.

TITA. I bet he is.

MEDEA. *Ai* Tita…that tongue…

TITA. But you trust him…

MEDEA. With all of my heart, I would die for him.

TITA. *Porque eres una ciega.*

MEDEA. Not blind.

TITA. Love is like a good *mole*, rich and delicious, but then it gets cold and you can't stand to look at him, I mean the *mole*…

MEDEA. My love is not *mole*.

TITA. *Ai*, Medea, you almost make me believe it.

The sound of a horn on a cart.
Ai! Josefina!

We hear a woman's voice yell out…
JOSEFINA. *(Offstage.)* MUÑECAS…

Tita yells back. Medea stiffens.
TITA. *AQUI ESTAMOS!*

She found us! This is the one I told you about that makes the sweet bread.

Tita notices Medea's apprehension.
Ai, don't worry, Medea, she's one of us, I promise. I asked her to

come, maybe she could be a friend. And don't argue with me, you need a friend. If you won't go out, then I will bring them to you…

> *Josefina, a no-nonsense street vendor, in apron, with a scarf on her head, appears. She holds a bag with* pan dulce.

JOSEFINA. *Hola viejita! Cómo estás?*

TITA. Doing what I do best, nothing!

> *This makes Josefina laugh. Medea stands in front of her sewing machine.*

Esta es mi Medea.

JOSEFINA. *Hola* Medea!

> *Josefina hugs Medea with abandon.*

Wow, you are so beautiful, I don't know why but I was expecting to meet an old *bruja* for some reason.

Tita told me all about you, but to be honest, I already knew. People talk about your gift. *La costurera,* oh wow! I'm from near you. Carapan.

MEDEA. Carapan!

San Juan Bautista.

JOSEFINA. Our patron saint, very good, but your people have *el guaco,* your own bird!

TITA. And the monarchs and the avocados…

JOSEFINA. No bragging *viejita*! Hey, did you hear they found a *guaco* out here?

MEDEA. They did?

JOSEFINA. Who knew a bird from our country could travel this far, but if we can, why can't our birds? I hope they're not as desperate as we are. I am so happy to meet you Medea, already you feel like family. I know some people from Zamora, but you know, our soccer teams, we should be enemies.

MEDEA. How do you know each other?

JOSEFINA. Oh, she comes to my cart almost every morning, we spend an hour gossiping, but it's never enough, right Tita?

TITA. I could *chismear* all day. Medea, the only way to see Boyle Heights is from the *pan dulce* cart.

JOSEFINA. It's true, I know everyone *en el barrio* now. *(Looks down at her hands.)* Oh forgive me, I must be nervous, I brought you some *pan dulce* from my cart!

I never see you on the street, so I am bringing the cart to you. Hey, wait a minute, this could be like a new kind of service, like *Chino* food or pizza—*pan dulce* delivered to your door!

MEDEA. *Ai gracias*, you shouldn't have. Jason, my husband, says we should watch our weight.

JOSEFINA. *Qué?* I think every Mexican woman should have a big ass. I do! We should look like the old country—plump and full of possibility. I know your husband.

MEDEA. You do?

JOSEFINA. *Bien conocido*, he's very charming *tu esposo*, he comes by my cart. Hey, when he was a kid did he tour with Ricky Martin?

MEDEA. What!

JOSEFINA. I knew he was lying!

MEDEA. You work all day?

JOSEFINA. And night. All I do is work. I get up at three in the morning to bake the bread, on the street by five, and then home by four in the afternoon, if I am lucky… I'm usually over on Cesar Chavez.

TITA. She doesn't know the *barrio*. She doesn't go out, like the mother *en esa telenovela* "Una Familia Con Suerte"?

JOSEFINA. You mean the one that stays inside her house all day and makes her poor little dog *Abeja* sad?

TITA. *Si, esa!*

MEDEA. Tita…

JOSEFINA. Oh, don't be embarrassed, Medea, when we come to this country, we become each other's family. I just met you and I already learned something about you. You are like my sister. Come visit me down on Cesar Chavez and you can see the *gabachos*, they call them "hipsters."

TITA. She sells every last *pan dulce, que no Josefina*?

JOSEFINA. Even the "hipsters" buy my bread. I wanted to charge all the white people moving into the neighborhood more money, because, come on, let's face it, you know they have it. But then my friend, Aurora, you know, the lady who sells the *tamales* in front of the bus stop at Mariachi Plaza?

TITA. *Si la conozco.*

JOSEFINA. She told me I could get a ticket for that! She says it's "discrimination."

MEDEA. Really?

JOSEFINA. In Mexico, I had two prices, one for the rich and one for the poor, and no one ever said anything. Everybody accepts it. But in this country, they want everyone to be treated the same, even though they know not everyone is.

MEDEA. I don't understand this country?

JOSEFINA. You know *esta* Teresa who sells the *chicharrones* in front of the metro stop at First and Soto? She told me the rich people in Bel Air make their dogs walk on two legs!

TITA. *No me digas.*

JOSEFINA. In little mink coats. I hope it is okay to say, Medea, but your husband, Jason is *tan guapo*, sexy.

TITA. He's not.

JOSEFINA. Is he a good lover?

> *Medea is caught off guard.*

Ai, don't be embarrassed Medea, we're open books, we have nothing to hide. Only people with money have secrets.

It must be a lot of work to keep a beautiful man satisfied. I prefer my ugly husband. The only one that wants him is me! No no, mine is good, but I have to keep pointing him in the right direction. *(Points downward.)* Poor thing, he's always tired.

MEDEA. What does he do?

JOSEFINA. He works in the fields, oh, which reminds me, I came with a favor, is that okay? I wouldn't normally, but you know, family. I bought a dress to seduce him with, but it's too big, could you bring it in for me?

MEDEA. Let's see it.

> *Josefina pulls it out of the bag.*

Oh… Put it on.

Josefina begins to undress in the yard.

Ai Josefina, you can dress inside.

JOSEFINA. What for? I do everything out on the street except make love. To be honest, I would love to do it outside. Between the Payless and the King Taco.

Josefina changes into the dress, she spins around in it.

TITA. A nun is more seducing than that dress.

MEDEA. Tita!

I can make you a better one if you want. I can already see you in it.

JOSEFINA. Really? Wow. I could pay you in layaway or give you free *pan dulce* in exchange.

MEDEA. Just pay me when you can.

> *Medea goes to the sewing machine and gets some pins and measurement tape. Tita pulls her milk crate over and extends a hand for balance as Josefina stands on it. But before she does, Josefina reaches over and hugs Medea deeply; she does something intimate and affectionate, like maybe fix her hair a bit.*

JOSEFINA. Thank you, sister.

> *Josefina gets up on the crate with Tita's help and Medea begins to pin the dress up.*

We should try speaking English.

TITA. No speaking English—this is America!

> *They all laugh.*

JOSEFINA. We need to learn it. I am losing too much money. Have you seen all the white people in the neighborhood? I'm learning how to make bagels now.

Oh, by the way, call me by my American name—Josie. I am trying to get used to it.

MEDEA. Okay, Josie…

> *Medea works.*

JOSEFINA. How is Jason's job?

MEDEA. Busy. Do you know Memo and Quique?

JOSEFINA. Of course, the laziest nice guys I know.

MEDEA. Jason got a promotion supervising them.

JOSEFINA. Ah ha! Good to know.

> *She reaches into her bra and pulls out a little black book with a pen and writes a note.*

They can finally pay their *pan dulce* balance!

MEDEA. I hope he gets another promotion, but with less hours.

JOSEFINA. Back home a promotion was less work and a few more *pesos*. Here you work twice as hard and lose your friends.

MEDEA. And what about your husband?

JOSEFINA. Gone, the whole season.

MEDEA. Where does he work?

JOSEFINA. Sometimes he gets a job in *Ventura*, but this time he is in Oregon.

MEDEA. Is that far?

JOSEFINA. It's another state!

MEDEA. Oh.

JOSEFINA. Picking, picking, picking. His specialty is blueberries, four gallons in one hour! But it's very hard on his back, he can't straighten up all the way anymore.

A very proud man who understands the honor of being able to work. I just wish for him that it wasn't so painful, the heat, the time away, his body…

> *Josefina breaks down and puts her hands up to her face. Standing on the milk crate, she looks like a saint. Medea and Tita look at each other.*

MEDEA. Josie, *que paso?*

JOSEFINA. I'm sorry, I usually cry in our garage. I must feel at home with the both of you. *Por favor*, don't tell anyone.

MEDEA. I won't, Josie.

JOSEFINA. I cry because I long for my own child, my own flesh and blood, but my husband only likes to make love on Saturday nights. He's been like that since I met him.

TITA. Forgive me for asking, but is he loyal?

JOSEFINA. Too loyal! I wish he would have an affair, but that's not who we are.

MEDEA. That's right, Josie. We are of the past, the old country. It's not here.

> *She touches her head.*

It's here.

> *She touches her heart.*

I understand.

JOSEFINA. I knew you would. A baby made from us.

TITA. Any child would make you happy.

JOSEFINA. Yes, but my Progeny. Isn't that a beautiful name? I saw it on a brochure at the Boyle Heights Clinic. That is what I would name my child; *Progeny Elpidia Alcazar Hernandez.*

My husband thinks it's too obvious, he prefers "Destiny." He say's it's a very American name. That's like a Disney name, right? I don't want my kid to sound like a flying elephant.

> *Josefina looks down at Medea.*

Down on the street, I hear the children playing… I shoo them away towards Cesar Chavez and the noise and the traffic… I know I know! Don't say it, I just heard that come out of my mouth and it sounds terrible.

MEDEA. I understand…

JOSEFINA. It's not for lack of trying. We try a lot, at least on Saturday nights.

MEDEA. Tita is a *curandera.* She can help.

JOSEFINA. You're a healer?

TITA. We will make you some herbs, a blessing for a baby.

> *Tita takes out a bird feather and does a blessing over Josefina while they talk.*

MEDEA. I will make you a dress a husband cannot resist.

JOSEFINA. But don't make me look like Shakira, okay? I want to be sensual, but *decente*.

MEDEA. It's all about the fabric, the stitch, the way it flows, moves, and gives life.

TITA. And it will be blessed.

JOSEFINA. *Muñecas*, I am very happy to know the both of you. To be honest, I don't have many friends, well any friends, all I do is work, I have customers, not friends, and I miss home so much, don't you?

TITA. Every day.

JOSEFINA. You remind me of Michoacán, Medea. I can see the land on you. Suddenly I am surrounded with family and our customs. I am in your debt, *gracias* my friends.

> *She breaks down in tears.*

Oh damnit, I swear, I only do this in our garage.

> *Medea reaches up and takes her hand.*

I wonder if I will never have a baby and spend the rest of my life in Boyle Heights pushing a cart and selling *pan dulce*?

> *Just then, a soccer ball bounces in. Followed by Acan. Josefina jumps off the milk crate.*

Acan!

MEDEA. You know my son?

JOSEFINA. Of course, he and Jason buy my *pan dulce*.

MEDEA. They do?

> *Medea looks at Acan.*

Los zapatos.

ACAN. Dang, man.

MEDEA. *Qué?*

ACAN. *Nada…*

> *Acan runs to a corner in the yard, takes off his shirt and switches from Vans to huaraches.*

JOSEFINA. Medea, he's growing so fast, what a tragedy.

Josefina reaches into her bra and pulls out a dollar, which she gives to Acan.

MEDEA. Oh, you don't have to do that.

JOSEFINA. Are you kidding me? This makes the obligation of work a joy.

ACAN. *Gracias, Tía Josefina.*

JOSEFINA. Josie! Say my name like a hipster.

ACAN. Josie.

JOSEFINA. He is everything, isn't he?

MEDEA. He is.

JOSEFINA. The reason we live. Why we endure the pain of this country. This is all we have, Medea, this hope. Don't ever let him go.

MEDEA. Never.

Josefina leaves as Tita ushers Acan into the house. Medea is left alone in the yard. She looks towards the big buildings, contemplative. She goes toward the edge of the yard, but thinks better and backs off.
Acan enters the yard dressed in his Donovan soccer shirt. He can tell that Medea has seen it.

ACAN. Please?

She looks at him, torn, but loving him.

MEDEA. *Gracias?...*

ACAN. *Gracias.*

MEDEA. *Axquēniuhqui.*

Yuck.

ACAN. *Lo puedo decir en Español?*

Medea shakes her head no. Acan grimaces, but says it.

Axquēniuhqui.

She smiles and he runs into the house.

Four

Jason steps into the yard, the wear of a workday under him.
Medea is waiting for him.

MEDEA. Let's make love out here.

    It catches him off guard.

JASON. Excuse me?

MEDEA. Let's make love out here.

    He looks around, as if a joke is being played on him.

JASON. In the yard?

MEDEA. You wanted to before.

JASON. Well, before it was late and I was horny. What is this all about?

MEDEA. I have a friend who has always wanted to make love outside and I remembered how we used to…

JASON. You have a friend?

MEDEA. Before we came here. We used to make love everywhere.

JASON. Because we had nowhere to go! It was a big country, Mexico. What about the neighbors?

MEDEA. We had neighbors back home.

JASON. We lived on a farm, all we had was God's eyes.

MEDEA. Are you ashamed of him now too, Mr. *Americano*?

JASON. God is looking at you, Medea.

MEDEA. He should, I look good.

JASON. Silly *niña*.

MEDEA. I don't want it to feel like a prison. I want to love in this yard and make it a special place for us. Like before.

JASON. Are you sure about this?

MEDEA. Nobody can see…

JASON. Tell me you can do this.

MEDEA. I think so.

He looks around the perimeter, horniness getting the better of him.

JASON. What the hell…

They giggle as Medea places a blanket on the floor. It's sweet and romantic as Jason begins to take off his shirt. They kneel on the blanket, like two young lovers and he slowly, cautiously almost, reaches out to gently touch her, softly kissing her. She is almost trembling.

I've missed you.

MEDEA. Me too.

They begin to kiss and touch, it's sensual and sweet, Jason is taking his time, very careful.
We can see in his ease and patience that he is a great lover. He attempts to take something off Medea, she is trying her best to be brave, but as it goes on, you can see that she is beginning to suffocate, it's too much and she quickly freezes up in terror, trying to just breathe.

I can't. I can't…

JASON. Okay…

MEDEA. I'm sorry.

JASON. It's okay…

The moment seems long and painful as they both get dressed.

Armida gave me another promotion. Half the day I am in the front office with her.

MEDEA. In the office with her, you don't think having a lady boss is strange?

JASON. She's older than me.

MEDEA. You are older than me.

JASON. It's not the same.

MEDEA. It's worse.

JASON. You have nothing to worry about, we like our women to be girls, then mothers, then grandmothers, and finally, saints.

MEDEA. And bosses?

JASON. They don't count.

Jason points to her breasts.

I promise that when these fall, I will make the trip down to kiss them.

They laugh.

She has big plans for me, Medea.

I told her that we own land in Michoacán…

MEDEA. Why would you do that? We don't own that land.

JASON. It doesn't matter. I didn't mention your brother.

MEDEA. Why would you say anything?

JASON. I had to… To get her to notice me. You think I'm the only one out there? All of a sudden, I wasn't just a worker, but a friend from back home. I told you it would open a door.

MEDEA. Be careful.

JASON. I'm doing this for the boy. Every nail I hammer, every wall I put up, every condo I build here in this country is for our son.

MEDEA. You don't have to tell her everything.

JASON. She's one of the biggest contractors in the *barrio*. She is counting on me. Months and months of standing in front of a Home Depot taking anything I can get, and now here I am. I can't let this slip away.

MEDEA. Don't get carried away, please, you know how you are.

JASON. I'm just lucky she likes me.

MEDEA. And don't flirt!

JASON. Whatever it takes…

He smiles, she frowns.

So what if she has a little crush on me, I know why I am doing what I do, for my son. Besides, she wants to meet you.

MEDEA. She does?

JASON. She treats me like family, like a son, Medea. She's not so disconnected from the old country that she doesn't realize she needs a man.

Medea rolls her eyes.

Oh, come on. You need a man, why wouldn't she? Look at these hands—less drywall, more paperwork. Look at yours. These hands are too special to look this way.

She is letting us stay here.

MEDEA. She is? Here? Why didn't you tell me?

JASON. Would you prefer to live out in the San Fernando Valley? You don't even know where that is, do you? I hope you never do.

You need to learn to be of this place, Medea. Learn how to be American. This *barrio* is going to look very different very soon. So should you. Dress like them. Learn to talk like them. Be like this place. And you will see, we can be in charge, for once. One day this dream will be ours.

MEDEA. I love you, Jason.

> *He kisses her softly on the forehead.*

JASON. Medea, there are things we have to do, to get ahead in this country. I want you to trust me.

MEDEA. I do.

JASON. I will do what is asked of me, for us, for the boy. There are going to be hard choices to make.

But no matter what, I want you to know your heart is mine always…

> *She reaches for his hand and places it on her chest. When she does, the loud sound of a heart beating can be heard.*

Five

> *Tita enters and a new narrative starts, the company shifts into a different performance style, aided by sounds and images.*

TITA. A year ago on a farm in Zamora, she says

MEDEA. *"Vamonos"*…

TITA. And off we go. To this America.

> *Jason grabs a backpack and a jug of water from the yard. Medea and Tita each grab a small duffel bag. Acan clutches a toy and Tita's hand.*

We walk to the edge of the farm. The four of us. Medea, Jason, *el nino Acan, y yo.*

Barely anything we own between all of us.
We leave it all behind.

I wear *mis tenis.* Some water, food, and a change of clothes, *es todo.*

Jason says…

JASON. "Don't worry, it's easy…"

TITA. A truck pulls up, old and beaten, like me.
No window, just a big box.

A truck for car parts and dead animals.
And still we get in.

Two men stand and look at us.
They are like us, but they are also them. *Narcos.* Killers of our country, they run everything now.

We lie to ourselves. We will carry something for them.

That is why this journey is cheap. But still more than we can afford.

Jason pays, like we are getting on a bus. But this is no bus.

"Two days," the driver says.

I look at Medea. She is more determined than I have ever seen her.

The four of us join two young men looking for work—Juan Felipe from our town—and a quiet man from Morelia.

I also see an older man from Guatemala holding a bible. He is already tired, traveled so far.
I look at him and worry. But I worry more for Acan.

We pray for a safe trip.

   They are joined by the actor playing Josefina.

A young girl runs up at the last minute, on her way to Arizona. She is alone. I say, "Sit with me."

YOUNG GIRL. *Gracias.*

TITA. The driver says, "Don't worry, I won't abandon you."

We don't know him and I don't understand why we would go in the middle of the night, but this is how it is done.

The road is full of bumps. We bounce around for hours. Filled with fear and dread. The driver sings to himself and perspires.

We are hot, sweating like animals, and burning up. No air in the back. I can feel that we are hiding our desperation. Please God, let the driver know what he is doing.

The old man holds his bible tightly.
The girl is afraid but tries not to show it.
We talk, look at each other, smile, distract, and slowly the heat and the sweat quiets us.

So hard not to know anything, we take small breaths in silence.

All day we are moving, moving, moving, the endless hours.

We stop for a rest and the driver opens the door.
We are all surprised. It is still light out. Our sense of time is gone.

The driver tells us
"We are going into the desert. We are near the border. Stay calm if we get stopped. I will bribe the patrol to let us go. This is going to be the hardest part. Drink water."

Even if I cannot see it, I can feel the desert.

Everyone is exhausted and struggles for breath.

You can see everyone's chest and stomach, up and down, trying to find and hold as little air as possible.

Maybe this is what the *narcos* do.
They kill you before you arrive.

I didn't even bring a feather! An offering. Protection. I am such a fool…

Time passes. Becomes desperation. We whimper.

Then the quiet man from Morelia pounds his fist on the wall of the truck. The driver stops. Unhooks the door and it opens widely. A gasp. We all breathe in the air.

The man from Morelia jumps off the truck.
"I'm done," he says. "It isn't worth it."

He starts walking away into the desert.
He screams to us, "I have a terrible feeling. Be safe…"

Seven of us remain.
The door bolts shut.
We drive and drive, the only hope knowing it has to end.

Panic. No air. We find small holes on the floor of the truck. We lie down and stick our noses and mouths on the tiny openings. Like pigs, cows, off to slaughter. You can hear us gasping for air.

Suddenly, the truck brakes quickly. We are quiet and trying to hear.

The doors open. It is night.

Standing and staring at us are soldiers from our country. They look at us. They are short, dark, and in their green fatigues. They hold guns and rifles across their shoulders. They don't say anything.

Suddenly, two jump in grabbing the young girl.
I try to hold on to her, but one of the soldiers slaps me across the face. She screams.
They pull her out of the truck. She is wild in her desperation.

I can see three of them dragging her off to the darkness of the desert.

> *The young girl, screaming, is dragged off by the soldier, played by the actor playing Armida.*

Her muffled screams. Unbearable. And then it stops…

We wait. Unsure of what to do. Do we run?

And then without warning they return.

Two grab Medea, who doesn't scream. She tries to hold her ground.

Jason, Acan, and I hold on to her.
A soldier holds a gun to Jason's face. He is crying. I try to push them away, but one points a gun towards Acan's head.

We don't know what to do. I can't let go of Medea.

> *Medea walks willingly into the desert with the soldier, where she is raped.*

We wait. And wait.
They do what men do and they leave them out there.
After a while, you can hear drunken laughter.
They come back with their flashlights. They look in the truck again.

One of the soldiers gives a nod to the men, and Jason and the other man run into the desert.

Meanwhile, the leader, a man who is a boy, jumps onto the truck. He moves closer toward Acan. I stand in front of him. He laughs at me drunkenly.

SOLDIER. "You are too old for me, *vieja.*"

TITA. I raise my hand. Two soldiers draw their guns. I scream "*AHMOTSIN!*"

He goes back a thousand years. His spirit understands. I don't take my eyes off of him. I am eating his heart and he knows it.

"*Tlen mo tokatsin?*"

I have become a serpent. I show him my teeth. His eyes widen in fear.

"*Quizazssssss!*"

He is shaken, unnerved, but…still the leader.
He feigns a laugh and jumps off the truck.
The soldiers slash the tires.
They take the *narco's* merchandise. And they leave.

> *Jason and Medea enter. He is holding her gently as she hobbles, limping.*

Jason returns, holding Medea softly. She is in shock.

The other man has the young girl over his shoulder. She is now a carcass. No one weeps.

I sing to Acan softly.

> *She sings a couple lines from a huapango-style song like "Cucurrucucú paloma."**

He never lets go of my hand.

We bury the girl in the desert. At least she gets rest.

We get the old man up and he lays his bible on her. I look at the moon. *Tlazocamati.*

> *Tita mimes picking herbs and sticking them in her mouth as she chews but not swallows.*

---

* See Note on Songs/Recordings at the back of this volume.

I go out into the desert and find our herbs. I make a concoction.

> *She spits it out into her hand and offers it to Medea, who drinks it.*

Medea drinks it. It kills the soldier inside her.

Morning comes. We begin to walk.

We walk for hours without talking or even looking at each other. The morning dew evaporates into thirsty afternoon. A lizard scrambles.

We find a shack. With water.
And a little stall for a shower.

I wash away some of the dirt
And some of the pain too.

But I still hear the girl screaming in the desert.
And I see the face of a soldier who is a boy. And the old man, I can hear him sleep, with the bible at his side.

I let the water run and my tears follow.

> *She begins to cry.*

Someone knocks, "You okay?"

"*Si, si*, okay…"

There is still more journey.
I ache just to think of it.

I keep thinking, they can never build a wall big enough.
They never will, but they will always try.

To walk in the desert is to walk everywhere and nowhere.
But…after a while… It is clear…

There is no sign, no line, no welcome.
We are in the other America.

> *We are back in Boyle Heights at the house.*

Six

The backyard is transformed for a party. The wooden table is covered with plates, glasses, and beers. Jason is dressed up. Tita has a rebozo *draped across her shoulders. She sits on her milk crate away from the table. Medea looks beautiful in a simple traditional* huipil. *Armida,* la mera mera, *is dressed in an elegant but simple shimmering striped blouse, skirt, and big heels. She is truly a* señora. *It is post-meal as the music fades to their laughter. They are all transfixed by a story.*

ARMIDA. Sometimes I scream to all the people moving into Boyle Heights—"You are welcome, *pendejos*! If it wasn't for me, you wouldn't have central heating."

Do they think all these apartments were born this way?

JASON. That's right.

ARMIDA. I'm not saying that to be arrogant. That is something you learn in this country—to take pride and credit for the things that you do. Back home we are taught humility and silence. That doesn't work here, it's a sign of weakness.

Everything changes.

Armida looks at Jason.

It's the one constant in this industry, remember that.

She gives Jason a familial pat on the hand and Medea notices.

Nobody cared about this *barrio* for years. The city fathers built four freeways through East LA, do you think they were trying to build community?

Armida reaches for a beer, but it's empty.

MEDEA. I'll get you another one.

Medea stands.

ARMIDA. No, you should let the *viejita* do it, that's her job isn't it?

Viejita?

JASON. Tita!

So, missus, what is the trick to getting ahead?

ARMIDA. Marry them.

I said to myself, "If I am going to move ahead in this country, I am
going to have to get me a *gabacho!*" I didn't buy him, I know that
must sound like I got married just to get ahead, but I promise you,
I loved him. Those things you cannot help.

MEDEA. You are married?

ARMIDA. Was. He's been gone almost ten years now. Rest his soul.

Medea and Armida both do a sign of the cross.

His name was Yaroslavsky. He was Boyle Heights before any of us
were here. But to me he was just Yaro. I used to take him to *fiestas*
just to show him off. He was my life.

You need something to get by. We all do. We sacrificed a lot. We
didn't even have time for children…

You can say that every building I own is a child of mine. They take
just as much energy to keep up.

I know I'm lucky. Drive by a Home Depot and see all those men out
front, and you will know that.

JASON. Missus, I've been meaning to ask you…

ARMIDA. Please…

JASON. How did you cross?

ARMIDA. I flew.

MEDEA. You flew?

ARMIDA. It wasn't like it is now. I bought a student visa and a
dress from Ann Taylor. Do you know what that is?

Medea shakes head no.

It's a dress for women who are in business, you can't spread your
legs, the skirt is too tight…

Tita finally hands her a beer.

Thank you…

And I had a certificate from Los Angeles City College, where I had registered by mail using a PO box, remember those?

No one knows what that is, but she continues talking.

When I landed at LAX, the customs agent was a very serious Polish man who towered over me. He looked like he worked in a prison. I gave him my student visa and he barked, "What classes are you taking?"

He was trying to make me nervous, but you see, the dress was firmly in place. I quickly shot back, "Business Management."

He wasn't convinced and he volleyed back, "And why do you want to take that?"

I smiled, looked him directly in the face and said, "So that I can be your boss!"

She laughs and takes a swig.

Nowadays, I have a cousin who walked through the desert, swam through the ocean, and still they caught her at a McDonald's in San Ysidro!

I told her she would have done better at the Olympics…

JASON. Missus, in my humble opinion, it's not luck, it's work.

TITA. *(To herself.)* Now he has humble opinions…

ARMIDA. I reel them in with a shot of tequila, some cleavage, and then…BAM! We do business! Enough about me, let's talk about that *mole.*

A proud Jason looks at Medea.

MEDEA. A family recipe.

Armida raises her glass.

ARMIDA. To Medea's family recipe!

MEDEA. They are Tita's recipes.

Armida turns to look at Tita.

ARMIDA. *Viejita,* you are the cook?

TITA. No, the slave *pendeja…*

MEDEA. TITA!

> *Jason stands up. Armida reaches for his hand and makes him sit.*

ARMIDA. Now now, *viejita*, you know that we don't have slaves in this country anymore.

TITA. Then how do you make your money?

> *Jason shakes his head in disgust, but Armida laughs. She looks at Medea.*

ARMIDA. I am sure she's worth all that, if just for the *mole*. *(To Tita.)* Why don't you come sit with us?

TITA. No.

MEDEA. She's of another time.

ARMIDA. Like you?

> *Medea is embarrassed.*

Is that why you fell in love with her, Jason?

> *He doesn't say anything, Medea offers.*

MEDEA. He fell in love with me because he thought I was a bird.

ARMIDA. *(Smiling.)* A bird?

JASON. It's silly.

MEDEA. Silly?

ARMIDA. Silly or not, I want to know.

> *Although hurt, Medea keeps her cool.*

MEDEA. No, he's right. It's "silly"… I am sure you have more important things to talk about.

> *Armida puts her hand on Medea's with force, there is nothing reassuring about it.*

ARMIDA. I want to hear it.

> *Medea looks at Jason.*

MEDEA. Jason and I grew up near each other but he went all the way to Irapuato to join the army when he was young.

JASON. I deserted.

> *He looks at Medea.*

It's okay, I told her. They thought I lived in Irapuato so it was easy to come back home.

MEDEA. He came back to Michoacán and hid on our little farm. He knew my brother. In Zamora there are a lot of farms, someone

always leaves you a little something to get by outside your door—
one day a chicken, another day a *tamale* still steaming from the pot,
but Jason was in love with the birds.

ARMIDA. A bird-watcher?

MEDEA. Just one bird, *el guaco*.

ARMIDA. The bird of Michoacán…

MEDEA. That's right, in the fields picking, he hears this call.

> *Medea cups her hands and does the most amazing bird call.
> It sounds like a song.*

Gwa, Gwa, Gwa…
During the day it is the music of the land, a *guaco's* notes travel far.

ARMIDA. I remember that.

MEDEA. A storm arrived and everyone was running to get under
a tree, but Jason hears the call of *el guaco* and thinks to himself "I
know that bird is hiding in a dry place and I am going to find it!"
He starts running towards the call and as he gets closer he sees that
it is not a bird at all, but me imitating *el guaco*. I was just a girl,
muddy, with no shoes, playing in the rain…

JASON. And already so beautiful and ripe for the taking.

> *Impulsively, Medea reaches over and kisses Jason on the
> lips, who becomes visibly embarrassed. Armida stares at
> her. Medea walks away from the table.*

ARMIDA. Okay, enough about birds.

> *Armida looks at Jason.*

Jason, can I have a moment alone with your little *guaco*?

> *Medea clearly does not want the moment alone, but Jason is
> dutiful.*

JASON. It's fine. You should talk. I should go be with the night crew.

MEDEA. Tonight?

> *Jason kisses Medea on the forehead. He hugs Armida. He
> looks at Tita.*

JASON. Tita, the plates.

> *Sensing something, Tita sits instead.*

TITA. No no, I tired…

> *Jason, disgusted, leaves. Armida looks at Tita for a moment,*
> *smiles, and then looks away.*

MEDEA. I didn't know you owned this building. Thank you for letting us stay here.

ARMIDA. I buy these properties but I never go in. Jason goes out to the sites and gives me a report. You're a beautiful young woman.

MEDEA. Thank you.

ARMIDA. You look like where we came from. It's very comforting. I see you and think about the part of myself that I have lost…

You know I have big plans for Jason.

MEDEA. You are like a mother to him.

ARMIDA. No. That is not how I work. He has a lot of potential. He is very willing. But the question is, are you?

MEDEA. For his success, always.

ARMIDA. What about yours? He says you are a legend in the *barrio* with your sewing. He showed me some of your work…

MEDEA. He did?

ARMIDA. I want you to make me something.

MEDEA. It would be my honor.

ARMIDA. But he says you don't get out much… We can set up a shop for you, rent-free. I just bought a strip mall in Montebello. I could put you between a 7-Eleven and a Subway sandwiches.

MEDEA. No, thank you.

ARMIDA. No?

MEDEA. It's too much, I couldn't.

ARMIDA. You need to stop thinking that way.

MEDEA. What way?

ARMIDA. Like an immigrant… The reason I ask is because every request I have for Jason will affect you as well. I am bringing him more and more into my business because he never says no. I am hoping that you will not either.

MEDEA. Well, he is very clear about the decisions he makes.

ARMIDA. He is very hungry. Are you as ambitious as him?

MEDEA. With all due respect, *Señora Armida*, I think it is a wife's duty…

ARMIDA. But you're not married.

MEDEA. Excuse me?

ARMIDA. You are not married.

MEDEA. He told you that?

ARMIDA. I don't mean to be cruel, Medea, my time is short. I don't tell stories about birds.

> *Medea is caught off guard.*

MEDEA. Forgive me. I don't understand you.

ARMIDA. You don't have to. Jason says you're not married.

MEDEA. I don't know why he would say that.

ARMIDA. I do.

> *Medea tries to recover. Armida looks over at Tita and smiles.*

MEDEA. We don't have a piece of paper, but we have something more important.

ARMIDA. What is that?

MEDEA. A child.

ARMIDA. That's when he should have married you.

MEDEA. That's not always our custom.

ARMIDA. A family from Zamora, your parents must have been praying for it…

MEDEA. I don't mean to be rude, *Señora Armida*, but family matters are personal.

ARMIDA. Jason tells me everything.

MEDEA. Not meant for strangers!

ARMIDA. I'm not a stranger, little girl.

MEDEA. I think we have spoken enough.

ARMIDA. All my years here, the hard work, would be in vain if I didn't make sure something survived, to live beyond me. Do you understand?

MEDEA. I think you should go.

ARMIDA. I will leave the house that I own when I am ready.

Just then, Acan runs in, dressed in his pajamas, kicking the soccer ball. This stops Armida in her tracks.

ACAN. Armida!

This shocks Medea and she looks at Armida, who smiles at the boy. Acan runs to Armida and hugs her.

ARMIDA. *Cómo estás, mi amor?*

MEDEA. Acan!

Armida does not let Acan go.

ARMIDA. Give him room to grow, Medea.

MEDEA. Acan…

ARMIDA. If you hold on too tight, I promise, you will get hurt…

Armida holds Acan in her arms as the lights fade. Armida leaves as Acan goes to a skateboard in the yard.

Seven

Medea and Acan in the yard. He is holding his skateboard.

MEDEA. Where are your *huaraches*?

ACAN. Dad threw them away.

Medea tries her best to keep calm.

MEDEA. Where did you get that?

ACAN. From someone…

MEDEA. Someone? *(Hesitant.)* You can tell me.

ACAN. Armida.

MEDEA. *Señora Armida.*

ACAN. It's just Armida, *Mami*…

MEDEA. She told you to call her that?

He doesn't say anything.

She's *Papi's* friend?

ACAN. I think so. We go to her house.

MEDEA. Her house? What do you do there?

ACAN. Play Wii.

MEDEA. Wii? What is that?

ACAN. You wouldn't know, you don't even have a cell.

Hey, do you want me to ask her if you can come to her house?

MEDEA. Is that all you do, play Wii?

ACAN. We swim.

MEDEA. Who swims?

ACAN. Me. Dad.

MEDEA. Does he work there?

ACAN. Are you going to ask me everything?

MEDEA. Does he, does he work there?

ACAN. I don't know!

MEDEA. What do you like about *Señora Armida*?

ACAN. She dresses funny.

MEDEA. She does?

ACAN. She wears all these clothes that shine with squiggly lines, even her swimming suit has shiny lines on it.

MEDEA. She swims?

ACAN. It's her house, what do you think!

Mami, I was thinking… Can you make her something?

MEDEA. What do you mean?

ACAN. A dress. With shiny lines on it, she would like that. Can you please?

> *It's too much and Medea turns away from him.*

Are you okay, *Mami*?

MEDEA. I have a headache.

ACAN. Try making her a dress, I bet it will make you feel better.

> *Medea does not turn back.*

Can I go outside?

MEDEA. Yes, go, be careful.

Acan gets on his skateboard and starts to roll away.

ACAN. Make her a dress!!

He is gone. Medea looks at Tita.

Eight

Tita gets the banana leaves from the yard and hands them to Medea. Medea turns and holds the leaves up.

TITA. Clear your mind.

MEDEA. The Four Directions, to the ancestors.

TITA. Who are you?

MEDEA. I am *el guaco*, the mighty falcon gripping my hurt in my claws. I must make an offering. I flap my wings and they reward me with the gift of sound.

TITA. You must come to *el conjuro*, clean, pure.

The jolting sound of the horn on Josefina's cart.

Ai, pinche Josefina, me asusto!

Medea puts down the leaves, defeated. We hear Josefina shout…

JOSEFINA. *MUÑECAS!*

TITA. I am getting tired of all that bread…

They turn and wait for her. Josefina enters with a bag of pan dulce.

JOSEFINA. *Hola* ladies.

Tita takes the bag from her and feigns surprise.

TITA. Oh *pan dulce! Gracias,* Josefina.

JOSEFINA. Josie, *viejita!*

Josefina hugs Medea.

Sister, I love my dress. When I put it on it makes me feel like I should be on television. Now, feel free to say no, I won't be hurt, but I brought some fabric for another one. Is that okay?

MEDEA. For a friend, of course.

JOSEFINA. Let me kiss your hands.

MEDEA. Don't be silly.

JOSEFINA. There's nothing silly about the gifts that God gives you, right, *viejita*?

> *Tita nods her head.*

You look tired Medea. If it's too much, don't worry about the dress.

MEDEA. I need to be busy, my mind fills with thoughts day and night. Sewing clears my head.

JOSEFINA. Oh! By the way, I talked to my husband! He agreed that when he comes back, we are going to do it more often, including Wednesdays.

TITA. *Que bueno.*

JOSEFINA. I even stopped crying. Apparently, I was much louder than I realized and I was waking the family that rents us our garage.

MEDEA. Good for you.

JOSEFINA. I changed my life once. I can do it again. I came to this country like everyone—to survive.

I put my head to the ground and worked, at first just in the fields, but then out of the blue, one night I bake an old family recipe for my husband, an *empanada de calabaza*. And he tells me I should sell some during the soccer games at *el hoyo*, and sure enough everyone starts buying my bread and I go from *empanadas* to *conchas* and before I knew it I had enough to buy my cart. And by the grace of God, no one hassles me on the street. I do have a sign that says, "All police eat for free."

TITA. She does.

> *She looks at Medea and debates telling her.*

JOSEFINA. Medea, you okay?

MEDEA. What do you mean?

JOSEFINA. I feel embarrassed telling you this…

MEDEA. You say what you need to, Josie.

JOSEFINA. They are talking about you.

MEDEA. Who is?

JOSEFINA. I am telling you this as your sister. Be careful *mi cos-turera*. Can I ask you something?

MEDEA. We have been open books, Josie.

JOSEFINA. Do you talk to Jason?

MEDEA. What do you mean?

JOSEFINA. Does he treat you like a husband from back home or do you tell each other everything like they do in this country?

MEDEA. I think so.

JOSEFINA. Has he told you his plans?

MEDEA. Yes…

JOSEFINA. And you are okay with them?

MEDEA. Why wouldn't I be?

JOSEFINA. Oh, I didn't realize you were so modern, is that why you never married him?

MEDEA. Who told you that?

JOSEFINA. You need the marriage certificate in this country, Medea.

MEDEA. Our faith is in each other.

JOSEFINA. That's not the way it works for us. The rules for people like us are very old and clear.

MEDEA. You are not being very clear, Josie.

JOSEFINA. What is Jason doing with Armida?

MEDEA. *(Afraid to taint her husband.)* He is her employee.

JOSEFINA. Is that what he says?

MEDEA. It may be just a job, but he takes it very seriously.

JOSEFINA. You don't have your immigration papers, do you?

MEDEA. Is that all the women on the street do, talk about each other?

JOSEFINA. Don't tell anyone, Medea. *En serio.* They will use it against you.

> *Josefina looks at Tita and Medea.*

You don't know what is going on, do you?

MEDEA. Josie! If you have something to say, just say it.

44

JOSEFINA. Even in a *barrio* like this, Medea, someone always wants to be king. A city, a *barrio*, a *rancho*, it doesn't matter, someone always wants to rule. And the truth is there is always someone like Jason, someone with his ambition, who wants it…but, *mi costurera*, I'm not sure they are offering you queen.

Silence.

I should go. Can Tita deliver the dress?

Medea goes to the sewing machine and begins to work. Tita looks at Josefina, who starts to go.

I said too much. That's the thing about this country, too many rules for speaking. Next time I'll make up the truth and I'm sure they'll make me president. I'll see you on the street, *viejita*.

Josefina is gone. Tita looks at Medea.

TITA. It's just the things they say on the street. I've heard it, but I don't believe it. If you believe it, Medea, then I will believe it too. You know Jason, he's nothing if he's not liked.

Medea stops sewing.

But he's keeping too many secrets.

Nine

Jason enters, dressed in a work suit. Medea is waiting for him.

MEDEA. Why are you swimming in her pool?

JASON. Who told you that?

MEDEA. Is that what you do for work?

JASON. Of course not. I am doing what she asks, Medea. What the boss asks for.

MEDEA. Does she care that you are married?

JASON. Why are you listening to what people are saying? Who is spreading all this gossip?

TITA. Everyone knows your *chisme, cabrón*.

JASON. *Callate la boca!* Stop filling her head with lies.

TITA. Not lies!

JASON. Don't listen to her, she hangs out in the gutter.

TITA. This man is filled with secrets, Medea.

JASON. The only secret I have is how much I do for all of us. You too, *chismosa*!

We all have to sacrifice. This is an opportunity that will not come again. You and I both know that. This is what we have been waiting for. Yes, she has me by the balls and she's going to make me work for it, but you know that I can't live with a foot always on my neck. You know that is not me. I don't have to be king, but something better than beggar.

TITA. She doesn't have the experience that you have, Jason. Can't you see that? She doesn't live out there like you do.

JASON. Is that my fault? You know I have tried, Medea. Don't make me feel bad for trying.

When Memo and Quique's wives went to work at the Holiday Inn, I told you to go. It wasn't just a job. It was a chance to go downtown, to see how it works, to make friends.

Your mind is full of thoughts because you lock yourself in here day and night.

MEDEA. I work like you, Jason!

JASON. Yes, and too much, Medea.

This is not a job for the city. We can't keep living in the past when the future is calling us. What we want is waiting for us.

MEDEA. This is more than what we ever wanted.

JASON. More than what you ever wanted.

What are you worried about? Her? Let her flirt, let her fall in love, it's a small price to pay.

Everyone pays in this country. My heart is here, with you, always. We've worked so hard for this.

> *Medea breaks down.*

MEDEA. It's too much.

Jason is surprised by the intensity of her feelings; he goes to hug her.

I have an idea…

JASON. What?

MEDEA. Marry me.

JASON. Medea…

MEDEA. Marry me. Make it real.

JASON. You're being silly.

MEDEA. It's just a paper, right? Most of the people here don't believe in it anyway. Some of them do it five, six times. If all they want is a contract, let's make one. Maybe then Armida will see us differently.

JASON. It's not like that.

Medea can't control herself.

MEDEA. Tell me you don't love her!

TITA. Medea…

MEDEA. TELL ME…

A beat. Jason sees her desperation.

JASON. I don't love her.

She breaks.

MEDEA. Thank you… Oh God, I feel so ridiculous right now. I'm acting like a little girl. I am sorry, but I can't control my feelings. I've become some jealous fool inventing things in my head. I hate myself for it. But…I can't help it. I am…so full of so many feelings.

A moment of embarrassment perhaps, thoughts running in her head, an immature idea.

Let's put a curse on her.

JASON. What?

MEDEA. Yes, *un mal de ojo.*

TITA. *Niña!*

MEDEA. Tita showed me how to do it once. She will suffer so she'll have to give you more power.

He pushes her away.

JASON. Why would you even think of doing such a thing? That's childish.

MEDEA. You said it yourself—she's ruthless. This will humble her. She will share with you even more. You get what you need even quicker. That's your plan, isn't it?

JASON. It's not like that. She's one of us, Medea, our *gente*!

MEDEA. She may be from back home, but she is not one of us.

JASON. She's a door, Medea. That's all she is. A door. What's important is that she has given us an opportunity, a chance, to get what we want.

MEDEA. Then, *un mal de ojo* for *Tía Armida*!

>> *Jason steps even farther away. Tita steps in.*

JASON. You can't do that, Medea.

MEDEA. Why not?

TITA. Yes, why not?

JASON. Listen to me…this is going to sound more ridiculous than what it is, but I promise you, it's not what it seems.

MEDEA. Tell me…

>> *Beat. He stares at her, sees her desperation. He cannot lie to her.*

JASON. I married her.

MEDEA. WHAT!

TITA. *Hijo de la chingada…*

JASON. It's not what you think. In name only! It was nothing. They do it all the time. She set it all up—? A business transaction.

MEDEA. Oh my God…

JASON. She's even going to give us some money for it! Lots of people do it, people who have never even met. It's just a way, to keep a business alive, a way to stay in the country.

TITA. *Qué te dije!*

JASON. It wasn't what you think it is. We went to a court building. Like getting a permit to build property. That's all it was. It was just like going to do taxes, a transaction.

MEDEA. Why, Jason?

JASON. She made me an offer I didn't want to lose.

She slaps him hard across the face. He takes it.

Once you realize what we are going to get out of this, you will forgive me. I know you will. Do you think anything in this country is free? It all comes with a price, Medea.

She can barely bring herself to ask. Jason glares at Tita.

MEDEA. Did you make love to her?

He can't bring himself to look at her. He can't answer.

GET OUT!

JASON. If she adopts Acan, he will inherit what she has.

TITA. *Nunca!*

JASON. It's just business. We put him on a piece of paper. It's that simple. Don't complicate it with your feelings, Medea. I haven't.

MEDEA. And what about me?

JASON. You will always be my wife.

Medea spits into his face, and without warning, Jason grabs her by the hair and drags her away from Tita, who screams.

(*In a rageful whisper.*) We all have secrets, don't forget!

Tita grabs the large rusted machete in the yard and moves toward Jason. More hurt than scared, Jason runs out. Tita looks at Medea.

Ten

Armida enters. Tita backs away.

ARMIDA. I want you out.

MEDEA. Out? Where will we go?

ARMIDA. That's not for me to answer, you just can't stay here. Not in this house. Not in this city. You need to disappear.

MEDEA. You invited us to live here.

ARMIDA. I invited him. Let's not make things ugly. We can shake hands, smile, and be done with it.

Armida goes to shake her hand. Medea backs away.

He's not yours to keep, Medea.

MEDEA. He is my life.

ARMIDA. Listen, I'm not blaming you. In this world, men are allowed mistakes. I didn't make the rules. I'll tell you what, name a price.

MEDEA. I could never put a price on our bond.

ARMIDA. He has.

MEDEA. I have his child.

ARMIDA. I am giving Acan his future.

MEDEA. Acan is staying with me.

ARMIDA. I want you out of here by tonight.

MEDEA. Tonight?

ARMIDA. This is not a hotel.

MEDEA. Where will we go…

ARMIDA. Acan is staying with us.

MEDEA. NO!

ARMIDA. Young lady, I am going to take you to court and make a case for why the child should not be allowed to stay with someone who has been living in the country illegally, when his father, recently married, is already working on obtaining the boy's citizenship. And let's not forget that you have been working without papers in a sweatshop you made in your house without the landlord's permission.

MEDEA. You will invent anything.

ARMIDA. I didn't create the laws of this country, I just use them for negotiation. By the way, I am taking the old lady.

MEDEA. Tita?

ARMIDA. We don't want Acan to suffer. He needs her. I am going to cut out her tongue. But you, I want you out.

> *Medea bows her head and drops to her knees, something very old, and sadly pathetic.*

MEDEA. Please…

ARMIDA. Don't do this to yourself, Medea.

MEDEA. I am begging you.

> *Armida reaches down and touches her face, pulling it up
> from the chin to look at her.*

ARMIDA. Look at me. We don't need your shame. I can give him
what he wants.

MEDEA. Please, I beg like a dog.

ARMIDA. Don't beg, it's pathetic.

MEDEA. I am pathetic. I am a wetback, *una mojada.* Show me
mercy. I need time. Just a little bit. A moment. Hours.

ARMIDA. It's too late.

MEDEA. I will give you anything.

ARMIDA. Anything?

> *Tita looks on in horror. Medea looks at her for a moment
> and then back to Armida.*

MEDEA. I will… *(Starts to cry.)* leave Acan.

ARMIDA. Very good.

MEDEA. Grant me a day. Let me go with my dignity, please.

> *Armida thinks.*

ARMIDA. It might be hard to believe Medea, but I was there once.
Where you are now… *(Exhales.)* One day. Twenty-four hours.
Make them matter.

MEDEA. Oh, I will.

ARMIDA. But if you are not out in a day, I will call the *migra* myself.
You are invisible now Medea. Get lost in this country.

> *Armida leaves and Medea rushes to her sewing machine, as
> she begins to furiously sew away.*

Eleven

*The sound of the horn on the cart. Medea is caught off guard.
Josefina enters.*

JOSEFINA. Oh, I am so happy you asked for me. I missed you, friends.

MEDEA. Josie, thank you for coming.

TITA. You're the closest thing to family. We have no one.

MEDEA. *(Desperate.)* Please, I need your help.

JOSEFINA. My friend…

MEDEA. Sister. I won't make it without you. I need a place to stay.

JOSEFINA. I thought you couldn't leave the house?

> *The thought of it happening hits Medea for the first time. She
> looks out.*

MEDEA. I am going to have to…

JOSEFINA. What did that bastard do to you?

MEDEA. He lost his way.

JOSIE. Medea, listen to me, you can't raise Acan here in the city on
your own. You will lose him, to gangs or drugs or worse. Please, go
back home. It's our country.

MEDEA. I can't. It's not mine anymore.

JOSEFINA. Why Medea? I swear, that is where you should be.

> *Josefina goes to her and kisses her hands.*

If someone like you, so much of the old world, can't go back, how
can I? Tell me what happened to you, I need to know.

MEDEA. I can't.

JOSEFINA. Please sister, if I am going to help you, I want to know that
I did it because you are family, and that we keep no secrets between us.

> *Medea turns to look at Tita, who comes to her and hugs her.*

TITA. Tell her. She is family. Let the secret that is Acat stay here in
this country.

> *A moment has arrived for Medea. Something clicks in her,*

maybe hurt. She pulls away and gives herself an ancient permission.

MEDEA. *Tla xihuallauh… Tlatecuin…*

She conjures.

My brother, Acat, my twin…was born three full minutes after me, but he inherited everything. That is because women do not contribute, we adorn, that is our country. I loved him. He was my equal, but he was born a man.

I took care of my father. I did everything for him and my brother. We fed the animals. We planted the crop. We were servants. Our land was small, but it was rich with resource, but he and my brother wasted it.

When *mi papá* got sick, we made a potion but it was too late. Cancer had spread through most of his body. In his last days, I soothed his fears, made sure he was comfortable. I can still see him on his deathbed, cigarette in hand, barking orders, hour after hour…

In his last moment, he pushed me aside and asked to speak to my twin. My brother ushered me out of the room. Even then, I could tell that something was changing in him, by the second. My father willed him the land, giving him everything that was on it, including me.

When he died, I wept for him, but Acat did not. No grief, just ownership. Everything was his and he knew it. Honestly, I didn't care, I knew we would go.

It was Jason's dream to come here, to *El Norte*. All I could think about was making his dream come true, this man who gave me so much happiness.

I went to tell my brother that we would be leaving, but he said that I belonged to the farm like one of the animals. What? I couldn't believe that came out of his mouth. We had never spoken like that, he was…my other. We shared a language.

We argued, we had never argued like that before, and then…he hit me. Hit me… He had never laid a hand on me until that moment. But, you see, I wasn't his sister anymore. I was property. And just like that, he said, "Get back to work."

He couldn't even look at me. It made me so angry. I don't know where it came out of me, my love for Jason, I guess, but I screamed at the top of my lungs, "I AM LEAVING!"

It feels like a blur now, but he grabbed me by the hair and dragged me out to where the pigs were and threw me in the muddy pen. I was in shock. He just kept hitting me… Slapping and punching, I didn't know what to do…

I ran to where the banana tree was, I could hear him close behind, cursing me. I was struggling for breath. It was as if a dark spirit was right there in front of me. I reached for the first thing that I could find, the *machete* we used to cut down the leaves…

JOSEFINA. *Medea, no…*

MEDEA. He said he would take Acan and destroy Jason. Our dreams… I was so afraid. I called on the gods and asked for protection. *Y nada.*

He lunged at me and I lifted the blade, to scare him…but all I could feel was the weight of his body against mine, my brother, my twin, Acat… His body fell, bloodied, and the pigs…they were so ravenous, they descended on him, I ran out…

I wanted to scream, but no sound would come out. It was as if I wasn't there at all.

JOSEFINA. Oh, Medea…

  It's as if a spell is broken. Tita goes to her.

MEDEA. *In lak ech.* I killed the other me.

JOSEFINA. You did what you had to do…

MEDEA. That night we left. Jason's dream. I wanted it for him so badly… He is my only love.

TITA. Even after what he's done to you?

MEDEA. I'll make him come back.

  Tita bows her head in disgust.

JOSEFINA. *Ai Dios…* Medea, my *corazon* is breaking. Please forgive me, but I can't help you anymore, my sister.

MEDEA. What?

JOSEFINA. I can't risk this. Jason is helping me to get a little bakery at a strip mall in Montebello. Armida owns the property. I can't be in the middle of things, you understand.

MEDEA. I don't.

JOSEFINA. Medea, you know us. In the end, we're tribal. How can I not want to help you survive this place? But, you need to understand how things work here. It's just the way it is here.

MEDEA. Josie, just go.

JOSEFINA. I can't risk this. It took me so long just to get this far. This is my dream, Medea.

MEDEA. *Pues, entonces.*

> *Josefina quickly leaves.*

Twelve

> *Medea goes into the house and returns with a box.*

MEDEA. Get yourself ready.

TITA. Are we going?

MEDEA. You are going to go to Armida's house. Josie gave you her address. Take a taxi.

TITA. You're going to let go of me, just like that?

MEDEA. Jason is right. I've been too selfish. He said it best—she is a door. That is what I am going to make her. You are going to deliver this gift, as a sign of gratitude for the few hours in this house that Armida has granted us.

Acan asked me to make her a dress. *A su estilo.* I made it of a fabric that glimmers and shines, something with movement for her...

TITA. *Por favor, guardate la brujeria.* I beg you.

MEDEA. Don't beg! We never will again. Armida has given us a gift, now we give her one back.

> *Did the box just move? Medea hands it to Tita.*

Go!

> *Tita leaves with the box in hand.*

Thirteen

Jason enters the yard. He pulls out a stack of money, folds it in half and hands it to Medea.

JASON. Let me know if you need more. Have the boy ready in the morning. You don't need to pack anything. He has better clothes at Armida's.

MEDEA. Even I know this is not how one succeeds in this country.

JASON. Medea, listen to me, the price you paid for coming here. I'll never be able to forgive myself for not being able to protect you. Never. But to come this far, even after all that, and not take what is ours, it would be a sin. I never stopped loving you.

MEDEA. I know.

Jason goes to Medea and kisses her.

JASON. *Me voy…*

MEDEA. I'll be waiting…

Jason leaves the house.

Fourteen

Silence. Time. Waiting. Tita walks into the yard, dazed and in shock. Drops of blood on her clothes and face. She looks up and sees Medea on the stairs. In another part of the stage, Armida appears with the gift box.

TITA. Armida opens the gift. A smile.

I'm so stupid, I think nothing of it…

The dress is so delicate and vibrant. Your best work, Medea…

Hundreds of threads, sitting side by side, shimmering, like rain on a sidewalk.

She is in awe of the construction. She makes me promise to thank you…

Then it hits me…but it's too late…

The dress begins to slither…

The movement confuses her. The threads are alive and quickly encircle her. They begin to squeeze. She panics and jerks, but their constriction holds her with a vengeance.

The ones in the middle tighten, and violently shrink her waist. She bleeds from her nose and mouth. There is nothing I can do. She is terrified and shrieking.

Jason runs in, the look on his face… All he can do is watch, it is happening so quickly.

Armida tries to pull the dress off her, but the seams strike her hands with their sharp fangs. She starts to convulse. Armida's body is exploding.

She tries to say something to Jason, she never takes her eyes off him.

A last breath. He pulls a handkerchief out of his pocket. He leans down and places it over her face and…kisses her.

MEDEA. What?

TITA. He starts to cry. He begs her forgiveness. He weeps like a little boy.

MEDEA. No…

TITA. *Me traicionaste!*

> *Tita walks up to Medea and slaps her. She goes out of the yard and down the street.*

Fifteen

> *Acan enters. He looks different, almost a completely new outfit.*

MEDEA. *Mocehui.* Let's do our poem.

ACAN. I don't want to.

MEDEA. *Qué?*

> *He goes into the house, a vision of his father, as he speaks…*

ACAN. Mom, speak English.

Slowly, Medea turns and looks up at the house. She begins to walk toward it, following after him. She looks at the banana tree, stops, and reaches over for the machete that sits next to the banana leaves. Slowly she climbs the stairs. There is tense silence. And then…

Mami?

Mami! No!

Papi! Papi!

Mami!

Nooooooo…

A bloody hacking sound. Off in the distance we hear Jason scream…

JASON. *(Offstage.)* MEDEEEEAAAAAA.

Jason bolts into the yard, desperate and out of breath. He pounds on the door, trying to kick it down. It slowly opens and Medea walks out, dazed, dripping in blood and holding the bloody machete. Jason backs away. Medea leaves the yard and Jason makes his way into the house, searching desperately.

ACAN! ACAN!

Jason, frantic, as we can hear him pushing and pulling at doors.

No… No…

And then a scream when he finds him…

MI HIJOOOOOOOOOOOO.

Epilogue

Jason enters, bloodied by his child. He falls to his knees in the center of the yard. Tita enters and watches from behind the fence. Josefina enters and watches from behind the fence as well.

Time passes. Day to night. Jason sits in the yard.

He looks up at the moon.

From somewhere deep in the barrio, *we hear a woman's voice answering back.*

MEDEA. *Gwa, Gwa, Gwa…*

We see Medea in flight, a dress of guaco feathers, her wings make a great sound. Medea looks out over the barrio. *And off she goes… The sound of flight is drowned out by the sound of a helicopter quickly approaching.*

End of Play

PROPERTY LIST
(Use this space to create props lists for your production)

SOUND EFFECTS
(Use this space to create sound effects lists for your production)

Dear reader,

Thank you for supporting playwrights by purchasing this acting edition! You may not know that Dramatists Play Service was founded, in 1936, by the Dramatists Guild and a number of prominent play agents to protect the rights and interests of playwrights. To this day, we are still a small company committed to our partnership with the Guild, and by proxy all playwrights, established and aspiring, working in the English language.

Because of our status as a small, independent publisher, we respectfully reiterate that this text may not be distributed or copied in any way, or uploaded to any file-sharing sites, including ones you might think are private. Photocopying or electronically distributing books means both DPS and the playwright are not paid for the work, and that ultimately hurts playwrights everywhere, as our profits are shared with the Guild.

We also hope you want to perform this play! Plays are wonderful to read, but even better when seen. If you are interested in performing or producing the play, please be aware that performance rights must be obtained through Dramatists Play Service. This is true for *any* public performance, even if no one is getting paid or admission is not being charged. Again, playwrights often make their sole living from performance royalties, so performing plays without paying the royalty is ultimately a loss for a real writer.

This acting edition is the **only approved text for performance**. There may be other editions of the play available for sale from other publishers, but DPS has worked closely with the playwright to ensure this published text reflects their desired text of all future productions. If you have purchased a revised edition (sometimes referred to as other types of editions, like "Broadway Edition," or "[Year] Edition"), that is the only edition you may use for performance, unless explicitly stated in writing by Dramatists Play Service.

Finally, this script cannot be changed without written permission from Dramatists Play Service. If a production intends to change the script in any way—including casting against the writer's intentions for characters, removing or changing "bad" words, or making other cuts however small—without permission, they are breaking the law. And, perhaps more importantly, changing an artist's work. Please don't do that!

We are thrilled that this play has made it into your hands. We hope you love it as much as we do, and thank you for helping us keep the American theater alive and vital.

Note on Songs/Recordings, Images, or Other Production Design Elements

Be advised that Dramatists Play Service, Inc., neither holds the rights to nor grants permission to use any songs, recordings, images, or other design elements mentioned in the play. It is the responsibility of the producing theater/organization to obtain permission of the copyright owner(s) for any such use. Additional royalty fees may apply for the right to use copyrighted materials.

For any songs/recordings, images, or other design elements mentioned in the play, works in the public domain may be substituted. It is the producing theater/organization's responsibility to ensure the substituted work is indeed in the public domain. Dramatists Play Service, Inc., cannot advise as to whether or not a song/arrangement/recording, image, or other design element is in the public domain.